THE COOK'S COLLECTION
❋

SUCCESSFUL
SOUPS

Author: Annette Wolter
Photography: Odette Teubner
Translated by UPS Translations, London
Edited by Josephine Bacon

CLB 4161
This edition published in 1995 by Grange Books
an imprint of Grange Books PLC, The Grange, Grange Yard, London SE1 3AG
This material published originally under the series title "Kochen Wie Noch Nie"
by Gräfe und Unzer Verlag GmbH, München
© 1995 Gräfe und Unzer Verlag GmbH, München
English translation copyright: © 1995 by CLB Publishing, Godalming, Surrey
Typeset by Image Setting, Brighton, E. Sussex
Printed and bound in Singapore
ISBN 1-85627-735-6

THE COOK'S COLLECTION
❋

SUCCESSFUL SOUPS

Annette Wolter

Grange
BOOKS

Introduction

Soups have a very wide appeal – there are so many different types and they can vary in consistency from the thinnest consommés to rich and hearty meal-in-one soups that border on the weight of stews. Most soups are served steaming hot, but some can be sipped refreshingly chilled. Soups fit many occasions. They can be just the thing when you are short of time and need a quick meal, or they can make a delightful start to a meal when you want to linger with friends over many courses. The recipes included in this book show just how wide-ranging soups can be, both in terms of the ingredients used and the types of dish you can create.

For all their tremendous variety, soups fall into two main categories. The first is the lighter type, which should stimulate the appetite without being too filling. The second, perhaps served with good bread and cheese, can make a quick and basic family meal in itself. Of course, there are recipes for soups that will fall into either category depending on the size of the serving. A thick, puréed soup, usually eaten with the family at lunch, can be just as suitable for formal entertaining if served in a smaller bowl, topped with a swirl of cream and chopped chives.

Fine ingredients, such as a home-made stock, fresh vegetables and herbs, a little wine or sherry and some interesting spice such as ground coriander, make all the difference to quality when making soups.

Dip into this wonderful collection and enjoy all the pleasures of soup making.

Each recipe serves four, unless otherwise indicated

Vegetable Soup with Courgettes and Tomatoes

1 large onion
3 cloves garlic
1 tbsp olive oil
400g/14oz courgettes
400g/14oz beefsteak tomatoes
3/4/1¹/₂ pints vegetable stock
¹/₂ tsp each salt and freshly
ground black pepper
1 tsp dried oregano
2 tsps balsamic vinegar

Preparation time:
1 hour
Nutritional value:
Analysis per serving, approx:
• 30kJ/74kcal
• 3g protein
• 3g fat
• 9g carbohydrate

Peel the onions and chop them finely. Peel and crush the garlic. Heat the oil in a large saucepan and fry the onions until transparent. Add the garlic and remove the pot from the heat. • Wash and dry the courgettes. Cut off each end. Cut lengthways and chop into medium cubes. • Make an incision at the round end of the tomatoes. Put in boiling water. Peel off the skins and chop, removing the midribs. • Add the courgettes and tomatoes to the onions. Fry them briefly while stirring. Add the vegetable stock, cover and simmer for 15 minutes. •Season the soup with salt, pepper, oregano and vinegar. •Serve with plenty of heavy rye bread.

Consommé with Ceps

1 bundle pot herbs
250g/8oz beef tomatoes
1l/1³/₄ pints beef stock
500g/1lb 2oz wild mushrooms
(preferably ceps)
2 shallots
1 tbsp butter
1 tbsp flour
1 tsp dried tarragon
¹/₂ tsp each salt and freshly
ground black pepper
Pinch freshly grated nutmeg
125ml/4 fl oz cream
4 tbsps dry white wine
1 tbsp chopped chives

Preparation time:
1 hour
Cooking time:
45 minutes
Nutritional value:
Analysis per serving, approx:
• 820kJ/200kcal
• 6g protein
• 13g fat
• 12g carbohydrate

Rinse and chop the pot herbs. Rinse the tomatoes and cut into quarters. • Bring the vegetables to the boil in the stock and leave to simmer gently for 1 hour. • Clean and wash the ceps and cut both the caps and stems into thin slices. • Peel the shallots and chop finely. • Strain the stock. • Heat the butter in a heavy saucepan and fry the mushrooms and shallots in it. Sprinkle with flour. Stir the mixture until it is smooth and then season with the tarragon, salt, pepper and nutmeg. • Add the stock. Allow it to come to the boil briefly, then reduce the heat and simmer for 20 minutes. • Stir the cream and wine into the soup and sprinkle with the chopped chives.

Consommé with Cellophane Noodles

1 thin leek
100g/4oz button mushrooms
25g/1oz butter
200g/7oz minced meat
$^1/_2$ tsp each salt and freshly
ground black pepper
1 pinch paprika (hot)
1l/1$^3/_4$ pints beef stock
100g/4oz cellophane noodles
Lemon juice
3 tbsps soy sauce

Preparation time:
30 minutes
Nutritional value:
Analysis per serving, approx:
• 1100kJ/260kcal
• 16g protein
• 14g fat
• 20g carbohydrate

Clean, rinse and dry the leek before cutting finely into rings. • Brush the mushrooms clean and cut into thin slices.• Heat the butter in a heavy saucepan. Fry the leek and the mushrooms over a high heat. Add the minced meat, pat it flat and brown on all sides. Season the minced meat with salt, pepper and paprika. Pour over the stock and bring to the boil. • Pour boiling water over the noodles. Drain them in a sieve and cut them at once into small pieces. • Simmer the noodles in the stock over a low heat for 10 minutes. • Flavour the soup with lemon juice and soy sauce and serve hot.

Our Tip: *It is of course possible to use lean minced beef (which has fewer calories) instead of the ordinary mince and any other type of noodles instead of the transparent noodles.*

9

Consommé with Austrian Biscuit Diamonds

750g/1lb10oz beef ribs
500g/1lb 2oz beef bones
2 carrots
2 thin leeks
250g/8oz celery stalks
1 bunch parsley
1 onion
2 bay leaves
1 tsp white peppercorns
Salt
2 tbsps chopped chives
For the biscuits:
2 eggs
1 pinch each salt and freshly
ground nutmeg
1-2 tbsps cream
3 tbsps flour
For the baking sheet:
Butter and flour

Preparation time:
30 minutes
Cooking time:
3 hours
Nutritional value:
Analysis per serving, approx:
• 1700kJ/400kcal
• 32g protein
• 22g fat
• 18g carbohydrate

Rinse and dry the meat and bones. • Brown the bones in a heavy saucepan. Add the meat and 3l/5¹/₄ pints water. Simmer the stock for 3 hours over a low heat. Skim off any scum in the first 30 minutes of cooking. • Clean the vegetables, rinse and chop coarsely. Peel the onion and add to the stock together with the vegetables, bay leaves, peppercorns and salt. •After 2¹/₂ hours cooking time preheat the oven to 225°C/450°F gas mark 7. Grease a baking sheet and dust with flour.• Separate the eggs. Beat the egg whites until stiff together with the salt. Mix the egg yolks, the nutmeg, cream and flour and fold this mixture into the stiff egg whites. • Spread the dough over the baking sheet to about the thickness of a finger, and bake in the centre of the oven for about 10 minutes until golden brown. • Allow the cooked

10

biscuit to cool slightly. Turn it
out onto a chopping board and
cut into diamond shapes.
Divide these between four
warmed soup plates. •Strain the
stock, season it well and pour
over the biscuits. Scatter the
chopped chives over the
consommé.

11

Consommé with Semolina Dumplings

500g/1lb 2oz beef ribs
2 beef bones for stock
1 bunch potherbs (carrot, onion, parsnip, leek)
$^1/_2$ bay leaf
1 clove
1 onion
200g/7oz carrots
1 leek
$^1/_2$ bunch chives
1 tbsp soy sauce
$^1/_4$ tsp salt
For the dumplings:
100ml/3fl oz water
25g/1oz butter
Pinch each of salt and freshly grated nutmeg
50g/2oz semolina
1 small egg

Preparation time:
30 minutes
Cooking time:
3 hours 10 mins
Nutritional value:
Analysis per serving, approx:
• 1200kJ/290kcal
• 17g protein
• 17g fat
• 17g carbohydrate

Stick the clove and bay leaf into the onion. Bring 2l/3$^1/_2$ pts water to the boil with the meat and bones, and the studded onion. Skim off the scum forming and simmer the stock for 3 hours. • Wash the carrots and leek and cut into fine strips. Cover the julienne strips and set aside. • To make the dumplings bring the water to the boil adding the butter, salt and nutmeg. Stir in the semolina. Leave to cool and to absorb the liquid for 10 minutes. Stir in the egg. • Strain the stock and season with the soy sauce and salt. Simmer once more. • Using 2 teaspoons form small dumplings from the semolina mixture and simmer these together with the julienne strips in the stock over a low heat for 10 minutes. •Wash and dry the chives. Cut into fine rings. Scatter these over the soup just before serving.

Consommé with Marrow Dumplings

750g/1lb 10oz beef bones for stock
500g/1lb 2oz best end of neck of beef
1 bunch potherbs (carrot, onion, parsnip, leek)
1 onion
1 tsp salt
1 handful mustard and cress
For the dumplings:
1 day-old bread roll
2 marrow bones
1 egg
Pinch each salt and freshly ground black pepper
2 -3 tbsps flour

Preparation time:
30 minutes
Cooking time:
3 hours
Nutritional value:
Analysis per serving, approx:
• 1200kJ/290kcal
• 27g protein
• 10g fat
• 18g carbohydrate

Peel the onion and bring to the boil 2l/3¹/₂ pts of water to which has been added the bones, the meat, the pot herbs and the onion. Add salt. During the first 30 minutes of the cooking, skim off the scum from the stock. Cover the pan and simmer over a low heat for about 3 hours.
• Soak the roll to make the dumplings. • Brown the bones in a pan until the marrow is loosened. • Squeeze the water from the soaked roll. Prepare a dough from the roll, the marrow, salt, pepper and as much flour as required to make the dough smooth. Form into dumplings the size of walnuts. • Strain the stock and bring to simmering point. • Let the dumplings simmer in the consommé for 10 minutes.• Garnish with the cress.

Avocado Soup

4 large ripe avocados
Juice of 1 lemon
¹/₂ tsp salt
¹/₂ tsp freshly ground white
pepper
1 pinch freshly grated nutmeg
1 bunch dill
750ml/1¹/₄ pints chicken stock
100g/4oz crème fraîche
4 eggs

Preparation time:
30 minutes
Nutritional value:
Analysis per serving, approx:
• 3600kJ/860kcal
• 20g protein
• 85g fat
• 4g carbohydrate

Cut the avocados in half and remove the stones. Lift out the flesh and purée together with the lemon juice, salt, pepper and nutmeg in a blender. • Wash and dry the dill and remove the stems. Crush the stems and cook them in the stock for 10 minutes. • Chop the dill leaves finely. Cover them and set aside. • Remove the dill stems from the stock. Add the avocado purée. Beat with a whisk to blend it and leave to simmer for 5 minutes. Do not let it boil. • Mix the crème fraîche with the dill leaves. • Separate the eggs. Place each egg yolk in half an eggshell and put this in a salt–filled bowl to prevent the eggshell from falling over. • Serve the crème fraîche separately. • Divide the avocado soup between four soup bowls and serve each with an egg yolk and some crème fraîche. • The egg yolk and crème fraîche are mixed into the soup at table in the desired proportions.

Beetroot Soup

750g / 1lb 10oz small beetroots
750ml / 1¼ pints chicken stock
1 tart apple
Juice of 1 lemon
250ml / 4fl oz sour cream
Pinch each salt, freshly ground
black pepper and sugar
1 bunch chives

Preparation time:
40 minutes
Nutritional value:
Analysis per serving, approx:
• 700kJ/170kcal
• 5g protein
• 7g fat
• 22g carbohydrate

Peel the beetroot thinly. Set one aside and chop the others into cubes. •Cook the cubed beetroot in the stock in a covered pan for 20 minutes. •Core the apple, cut into quarters, grate it coarsely and mix with the lemon juice. • Grate the remaining beetroot finely. • Set aside 4 tbsps of the sour cream. • Purée the cooked beetroot in the blender. Mix them with the sour cream. Reheat the soup and season it with salt, pepper and sugar. •Wash and dry the chives and chop finely. • Stir the grated apple and beetroot into the soup. Pour on the remaining sour cream and sprinkle with chives before serving.

Our tip: *The soup is a little richer if you use whipping cream, whipped until semi-stiff, instead of sour cream.*

Pumpkin Soup Served in the Pumpkin Shell

1 pumpkin, approximately
1.5kg/3³/₄lbs
1 large onion
1 small fennel
60g/2¹/₂oz butter
1 tsp salt
¹/₄ tsp freshly ground white
pepper
200ml/6fl oz cream
Some milk if necessary
4 tbsps pumpkin seeds

Preparation time:
1¹/₄ hours
Nutritional value:
Analysis per serving, approx:
• 1800kJ/430kcal
• 8g protein
• 34g fat
• 21g carbohydrate

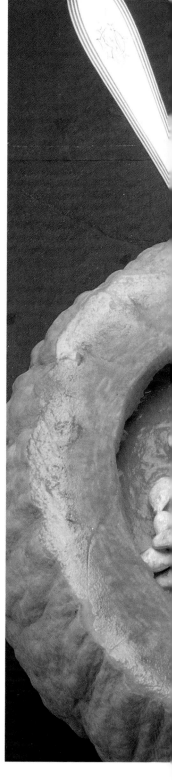

Preheat the oven to 50°C/120°F/ Gas Mark 1.
• Rinse and dry the pumpkin. Cut off the upper third at the stem end to form a lid. • At the lower end cut off a 2cm/³/₄-inch strip to ensure that the shell does not roll over sideways. Now warm the pumpkin in the oven without its lid. • Peel the onion and chop finely. Wash and clean the fennel and cut into strips. •Melt half the butter in a large casserole and fry the chopped onion and fennel until golden. Add the pumpkin flesh, 250ml/8fl oz water, half the salt and pepper, cover the pan and cook over a low heat for 30 minutes. • Purée the soup either by using a fine sieve or by liquidising in a blender, and fold in the cream. If the soup is too thick, thin it with a little milk. • Season the soup well with the remaining salt and pepper. • Heat the rest of the butter in the pan and fry the pumpkin seeds, stirring frequently, until golden brown. • Serve the soup in the heated pumpkin and sprinkle with the fried seeds.

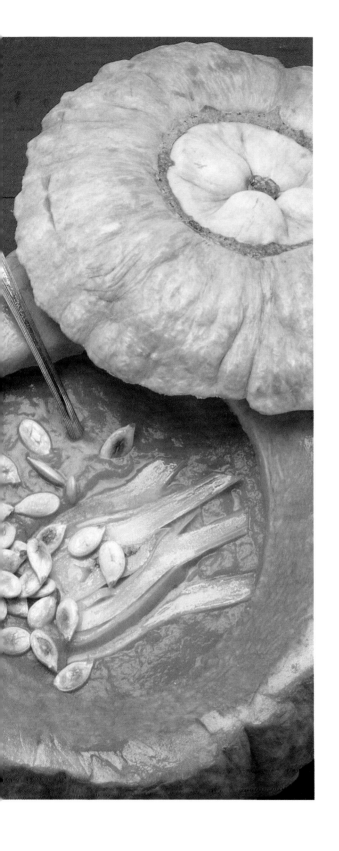

Swedish Vegetable Soup

750g/1lb10oz fresh spring vegetables (carrots, peas, mangetout, cauliflower, Swiss chard, new potatoes, etc).
500ml/18fl oz vegetable stock
500ml/18fl oz full cream milk
1/2 tsp sea salt
Pinch freshly grated nutmeg
1/2 bunch each dill, chervil and parsley

Preparation time:
45 minutes
Nutritional value:
Analysis per serving, approx:
- 660kJ/160kcal
- 10g protein
- 5g fat
- 18g carbohydrate

Peel or scrape the vegetables, wash and cut them into cubes. • Cook the vegetables in the vegetable stock and milk in a covered pan for 10-15 minutes. • Season the soup with the salt and nutmeg and keep it hot. • Wash and dry the herbs. Remove the coarser stems and chop the rest of the herbs finely. • Serve the soup sprinkled with the chopped herbs.

Our Tip: This soup can be prepared with whichever vegetables are in season. Green beans, kohlrabi, courgettes, asparagus, tender spinach leaves and tomatoes can all be used in the mixture. In the autumn you could try making the soup with tender white cabbage, turnips and broccoli.

Mushroom and Cheese Soup

250g/8oz mushrooms
1 onion
200g/7oz cheese spread
50g/2oz cheese and mushroom
spread
3 tbsps butter
2 tbsps flour
1l/1³/₄ pints milk
Pinch each cayenne and freshly
grated nutmeg
¹/₂ bunch parsley

Preparation time:
30 minutes
Nutritional value:
Analysis per serving, approx:
• 1800kJ/430kcal
• 21g protein
• 31g fat
• 18g carbohydrate

Wash the mushrooms, drain and cut into thin slices. • Peel the onion and chop finely. • Cut the creamy cheeses into small cubes. • Heat the butter in a large saucepan and fry the mushrooms and onion until they are straw coloured. Then stir in the flour. Gradually add the milk and the cheese cubes. • Bring the soup to the boil then cook it gently, stirring constantly, until the cheese has melted. • Season the soup with the cayenne and nutmeg. Wash and dry the parsley. Chop it and sprinkle over the soup.

Cream of Asparagus Soup with Prawns

3 shallots
500g/1lb 2oz green asparagus
25g/1oz butter
750ml/1¼ pints vegetable stock
125ml/4fl oz cream
1/4 tsp each salt and freshly ground white pepper
3 tbsps dry white wine
Pinch freshly grated nutmeg
100g/4oz prawns
Some chervil leaves

Preparation time:
1 hour
Nutritional value:
Analysis per serving, approx:
• 730kJ/170kcal
• 8g protein
• 15g fat
• 4g carbohydrate

Peel the shallots and chop finely. • Peel the asparagus stalks carefully. Remove the tough ends. Chop the asparagus into approximately 4cm/1¾-inch pieces. • Heat a tablespoon of butter in a large saucepan and fry the chopped shallots until transparent. Add the pieces of asparagus and continue cooking, stirring frequently, over a low heat for 10 minutes. •Add the stock, cover the pan and cook the asparagus over a gentle heat for 15 minutes. • Blend the soup in a liquidiser and return it to the pan. Fold in the cream, cover the pan and simmer for a further 15 minutes. • Season the soup with the salt, pepper, wine and nutmeg. • Heat the remaining butter in a pan over a high heat. Heat the prawns by tossing in the hot butter. • Preheat four bowls or soup plates and ladle the asparagus soup into them, garnishing each portion with prawns and chervil leaves.

Cream of Radish Soup

1 onion
2-3 bunches radishes,
depending on their size
100g/4oz full-fat cream cheese
100g/4oz crème fraîche
25g/1oz butter
750ml/1¼ pints chicken stock
½ tsp each salt and freshly
ground white pepper
Pinch each cayenne and freshly
grated nutmeg
Juice of 1 lemon

Preparation time:
45 minutes
Nutritional value:
Analysis per serving, approx:
• 1100kJ/260kcal
• 5g protein
• 24g fat
• 6g carbohydrate

Peel the onion and chop
finely. • Wash the radishes
carefully together with their
leaves. Reserve a few of the
better leaves. • Blend the
radishes with the remaining
leaves, the crème fraîche and
the cream cheese in the
liquidiser. • Heat the butter in
a large casserole and fry the
onion until transparent. Stir in
the blended radish and the
chicken stock, cover and cook
over a low heat for 20
minutes. • Cut the remaining
radish leaves into fine strips. •
Season the soup well with the
salt, pepper, cayenne, nutmeg
and lemon juice. Serve
sprinkled with the radish
leaves.

*Our Tip: This soup is also
delicious cold. It makes a refreshing
snack on a summer's day.*

Tuscan Tomato Soup

1 onion
2 red peppers
1 celery stalk
750g/1lb 10oz beefsteak
tomatoes
2 tbsps olive oil
750ml/1¼ pints beef stock
1 pinch freshly ground black
pepper
4 eggs
60g/2½ oz Parmesan cheese
8 slices French bread

Preparation time:
50 minutes
Nutritional value:
Analysis per serving, approx:
• 1900kJ/450kcal
• 26g protein
• 21g fat
• 38g carbohydrate

Peel and chop the onion. Wash and dry the red peppers. Cut them in half. Remove their cores then slice them lengthways into thin strips. • Remove the green leaves from the celery. Wash and set them aside. Clean and wash the celery and cut in slices. • Blanch and skin the tomatoes, then cut into cubes. •Heat the oil in a large saucepan. Fry the chopped onion until transparent. Add the remaining vegetables and sweat over a low heat for 10 minutes. • Heat the stock and pour over the vegetables. Cover and simmer for 15 minutes. Season with the pepper. • Break the eggs into a bowl. Grate the cheese and whisk with the eggs. • Grill the bread slices lightly on both sides and divide between four soup bowls. • Remove the soup from the heat. Stir in the egg and cheese mixture. Pour over the bread and serve sprinkled with the celery leaves.

Tomato Soup with Pumpkin

750g/1lb 10oz beefsteak
tomatoes
1 tsp dried thyme
Some celery leaves
1 onion
1 garlic clove
1 tbsp olive oil
25g/1oz butter
1¹/₂ tbsps flour
Generous pinch each salt and
sugar
1 tsp chicken stock granules
dash of Tabasco sauce
200g/7oz canned or cooked
pumpkin
100ml/3fl oz whipping cream
¹/₂ tsp coarsely ground white
pepper
2 sprigs basil

Preparation time:
50 minutes
Nutritional value:
Analysis per serving, approx:
• 850kJ/220kcal
• 4g protein
• 15g fat
• 14g carbohydrate

Quarter the tomatoes. Bring 750ml/1¹/₄ pints water to the boil and simmer the tomatoes, thyme and celery leaves for 25 minutes. • Peel and chop the onion and garlic. • Sieve the tomatoes. • Heat the butter and oil and fry the onion and garlic until transparent. Dust with flour and fry until light brown. • Slowly add the puréed tomatoes to the roux. Season with salt, sugar, stock granules and Tabasco sauce. • Cover and simmer for a little longer. • Add the canned pumpkin to the soup. • Whip the cream until stiff and season with pepper. • Wash and dry the basil leaves. • Ladle the soup into serving bowls and garnish with the peppered cream and basil leaves.

Cream of Corn Soup

1 onion
2 tbsps oil
400g/14oz corn, frozen or canned
750ml/1¼ pints beef stock
250ml/8fl oz sour cream
½ tsp each salt and freshly ground black pepper
Pinch chilli powder
100g/4oz smoked boiling sausage
1 bunch chives

Preparation time:
30 minutes
Nutritional value:
Analysis per serving, approx:
• 1500kJ/360kcal
• 10g protein
• 24g fat
• 25g carbohydrate

Peel the onion and chop finely. • Heat the oil in a large casserole and fry the onion until transparent. • Add the corn and, if using the frozen variety, fry briefly. Add the stock and cook the corn in a covered pan over a low heat for 10 minutes. • Blend the corn in the liquidiser and pass through a fine sieve to remove any of the skins. Return the purée to the casserole. Add half the sour cream and heat the soup without letting it boil so that the cream does not curdle. • Season the soup well with salt, pepper and chilli powder. • Skin the smoked boiling sausage and cut into thin slices. Fry these in a dry pan until crisp. • Wash and dry the chives before chopping finely. Preheat some soup bowls. Serve the soup, adding the sausage slices and the remaining sour cream in the centre of each bowl. Sprinkle with chopped chives.

Cream of Peppers Soup

700g/1lb 9oz green peppers
3 cloves garlic
3 shallots
25g/1oz butter
Just under 1l/1³/4 pints beef stock
100g/4oz double cream
¹/2 tsp each salt and freshly ground white pepper
Pinch chilli powder
2 tsps balsamic vinegar
1 tbsp chopped parsley

Preparation time:
45 minutes
Nutritional value:
Analysis per serving, approx:
• 1000kJ/240kcal
• 4g protein
• 21g fat
• 9g carbohydrate

Wash and dry the peppers. Cut into quarters and remove the stems and white insides. Put one pepper aside and cut the remaining ones into strips. •Peel the garlic. Peel the shallots and chop finely. • Melt the butter in a large casserole. Fry the shallots until transparent. Crush the garlic. Add this and the paprika strips to the shallots and fry for 5 minutes. • Add the beef stock to the vegetables. Cover the pan and cook for 20 minutes over a low heat. • Chop the remaining pepper into ¹/2cm/¹/4-inch cubes. •Blend the cooked peppers in the liquidiser. Return to the pan and fold in the double cream. • Season the soup with the salt, pepper, chilli powder and vinegar and reheat it. • Preheat some soup plates or bowls. Serve the soup garnished with the green pepper cubes and parsley. Delicious with fresh bread and chilled butter.

Cream of Mushroom Soup

1 small onion
350g/11oz oyster mushrooms
25g/1oz butter
100g/4oz crème fraîche
5 tbsps dry sherry
750ml/1¼ pints chicken stock
¼ tsp each salt and freshly
ground white pepper
Pinch cayenne
1 tsp pink peppercorns
Bunch of chervil

Preparation time:
30 minutes
Nutritional value:
Analysis per serving, approx:
• 850kJ/200kcal
• 4g protein
• 16g fat
• 3g carbohydrate

Peel and chop the onion. •
Remove any tough fibres
from the oyster mushrooms,
rinse, leave to drain and cut
into thin strips. • Melt the
butter in a large saucepan and
fry the chopped onions until
transparent. • Add the
mushrooms and stir-fry until
all the liquid has evaporated. •
Stir in the crème fraîche and
sherry and then purée in a
blender. • Return the puréed
vegetables to the saucepan, add
the chicken stock and bring to
the boil. • Season with salt,
pepper and cayenne. Keep
warm. • Crush the pink
peppercorns. • Serve the soup
sprinkled with pink
peppercorns and chervil.

Our tip: *Try using fresh
pomegranate seeds, if the flavour of
pink peppercorns is too strong.*

Chicory Soup with Peas

2 spring onions
300g/10oz chicory
25g/1oz butter
300g/10oz shelled or frozen peas
125ml/4fl oz dry white wine
750ml/1¼ pints beef stock
½ tsp each salt and freshly ground white pepper
Juice of ½ lemon
100g/4oz cooked ham , rind removed
Bunch of chervil

Preparation time:
30 minutes
Nutritional value:
Analysis per serving, approx:
• 750kJ/180kcal
• 11g protein
• 8g fat
• 11g carbohydrate

Rinse, trim and chop the spring onions. • Rinse the chicory, discarding the outer leaves. Cut out a wedge from the base as most of the bitterness is concentrated here. Cut the heads into strips. • Melt the butter in a large saucepan and fry the onion rings for 2 minutes, stirring frequently. • Add the peas, white wine and stock. Cover and simmer for 10 minutes. • Stir the chicory into the soup and season with salt, pepper and lemon juice. • Cut the ham into strips. • Wash the chervil, drain and remove the stalks • Serve the soups garnished with chervil and strips of ham.

Minestrone Verdura

To serve 8:
125g/5oz borlotti beans
125g/5oz pancetta or green bacon
2 onions
2 carrots
200g/7oz celery
1 leek
150g/5¹/₂oz French beans
300g/10oz Savoy cabbage
2 small courgettes
250g/8oz potatoes
2 tbsps tomato purée
1 tsp salt
2 generous pinches freshly ground white pepper
2 garlic cloves
75g/3oz short-grain rice
Bunch of parsley, chopped
75g/3oz grated Parmesan cheese

Soaking time:
12 hours
Preparation time:
1¹/₂ hours
Nutritional value:
Analysis per serving, approx:
• 900kJ/210kcal
• 11g protein
• 9g fat
• 23g carbohydrate

Cover the beans with water and soak for 12 hours. • Bring 1¹/₂l/2¹/₂ pints water to the boil and simmer the beans for 30 minutes. • Chop the bacon. • Peel and chop the onions, carrots, celery and leek. Trim the French beans and break each one into three. Slice the Savoy cabbage, courgettes and peeled potatoes. • Gently fry the bacon and then add the chopped onions, carrots, leek and celery and fry for 5 minutes. Stir in the tomato purée and then add to the beans, together with the French beans, salt and pepper. Simmer for 30 minutes. • Peel and crush the garlic cloves. •

Add the remaining vegetables, garlic and rice to the soup. Boil for a further 20 minutes. • Serve the soup garnished with parsley and Parmesan cheese.

28

Chinese-style Vegetable Soup

25g/1oz dried Chinese
mushrooms
40g/1¹/₄oz cellophane noodles
250g/8oz carrots
4 spring onions
2 tbsps sesame oil
1 tsp each honey, curry powder
and cornflour
750ml/1¹/₄ pints hot chicken
stock
150g/5¹/₂oz mung bean
sprouts
1 tbsp soy sauce or sherry
Generous pinch each salt and
freshly ground white pepper

Preparation time:
45 minutes
Nutritional value:
Analysis per serving, approx:
• 510kJ/120kcal
• 3g protein
• 5g fat
• 14g carbohydrate

Soak the mushrooms and
noodles separately in warm
water for at least 10 minutes.
Change the mushroom water
once or twice. • Peel the
carrots and cut into julienne
strips. • Trim and chop the
spring onions. • Heat the oil
and fry the prepared
vegetables. Stir in the honey,
curry powder, the drained
mushrooms and cornflour. Add
the hot chicken stock, cover
and simmer for 5 minutes. •
Rinse the bean sprouts in cold
water, add to the soup and
cook for a further 5 minutes. •
Break the drained transparent
noodles into smaller lengths
and cook for 2 minutes in the
soup. • Season with soy sauce,
salt and pepper and serve.

Hot and Sour Soup

20g/1oz dried Chinese
mushrooms
500g/1lb 2oz chicken giblets
and trimmings
1 onion
$^1/_2$ tsp salt
10 white peppercorns
250g/8oz pork escalopes
200g/7oz bamboo shoots
4 eggs
250g/8oz soya bean sprouts
4 spring onions
2 tbsps vinegar
1 tbsp soy sauce
Generous pinch of chilli powder

Preparation time:
30 minutes
Cooking time:
1 hour
Nutritional value:
Analysis per serving, approx:
• 1900kJ/450kcal
• 58g protein
• 21g fat
• 7g carbohydrate

Soak the mushrooms in
warm water. Wash the
chicken giblets and trimmings.
• Peel the onion. Bring 1l/1$^3/_4$
pints salted water to the boil
and add the onion, chicken
and peppercorns. Cover and
simmer for 1 hour. Scoop off
any froth that forms on the
surface. • Cut the pork and
bamboo shoots into strips. •
Beat the eggs. Rinse the bean
sprouts in cold water. • Trim
the spring onions, discarding
the dark green leaves and cut
into rings. • Separate the
mushroom stalks and caps and
cut into strips. • Strain the
chicken stock, return to the
boil and simmer the pork and
mushrooms for 3 minutes. •
Stir in the beaten eggs and
leave them to thicken the
soup. Add all the other
ingredients, heat through and
season with chilli powder.

Potato Soup with Croûtons

500g/1lb 2oz floury potatoes
1 bunch of potherbs (carrot,
onion, leek, parsnip)
1 onion
2 cloves
1l/1³/₄ pints beef stock
2 leeks
2 carrots
300g/10oz celery
25g/1oz butter
250ml/8fl oz cream
2 tsps fresh marjoram
Salt and freshly ground black
pepper
4 slices white bread

Preparation time:
1 hour
Nutritional value:
Analysis per serving, approx:
• 1900kJ/450kcal
• 11g protein
• 26g fat
• 47g carbohydrate

Peel the potatoes and trim the pot herbs, rinse and chop all these coarsely. • Peel the onion and stud with cloves. Simmer the potatoes, pot herbs and studded onion in the beef stock. • Rinse, peel and trim the leeks, carrot and celery. Dice or cut into rings. • Heat a tablespoon of butter in a saucepan and gently fry the vegetables. Add the cream, cover, and cook gently for 15 minutes. • Remove the studded onion, purée it in a blender, add to the soup and simmer for 5 minutes. • Season the soup with marjoram, salt and pepper. • Cut the crust off the slices of bread, cube and fry in the remaining butter until golden brown. Ladle the soup into serving bowls and serve the croûtons separately.

Celery and Potato Soup

500g/1lb 2oz celery
750g/1lb 10oz floury potatoes
1 large onion
50g/2oz butter
1l/1³/₄ pints chicken stock
Salt and freshly ground white pepper
1 tbsp lemon juice
Pinch of sugar
2 tbsps sunflower seeds

Preparation time:
45 minutes
Nutritional value:
Analysis per serving, approx:
• 1100kJ/260kcal
• 7g protein
• 11g fat
• 30g carbohydrate

Clean and trim the celery stalks. Rinse and peel the potatoes. Coarsely grate the potatoes and half the celery. Cut the rest of the celery into matchstick-sized strips and set aside. • Peel and chop the onion. • Melt 3 tablespoons of butter in a large saucepan and fry the onion until transparent. Add the vegetables and stir-fry for 5 minutes. Add the stock. • Cover and simmer for 15 minutes. • Season the soup with salt, pepper, sugar and lemon juice. • Fry the sunflower seeds and reserved celery strips in the remaining butter. • Pour the soup into a dish and serve sprinkled with the sunflower seeds and celery.

Kremser Riesling Soup

Quantities for 6 servings:
4 shallots
500ml/18fl oz Austrian Riesling or other Riesling
500ml/18fl oz rich veal stock
1 cinnamon stick
3 cloves
400ml/14fl oz whipping cream
$^1/_2$ tsp each salt, sugar and freshly ground white pepper
Pinch of cardamom
Ground cinnamon (optional)

Preparation time:
50 minutes
Nutritional value:
Analysis per serving, approx:
• 1200kJ/290kcal
• 2g protein
• 21g fat
• 6g carbohydrate

Peel and quarter the shallots. Bring the wine and stock to the boil and simmer with the crushed cinnamon stick and cloves. • Cover and simmer for 30 minutes. • Whip the cream until stiff. • Strain the soup and then slowly fold in the whipped cream with a whisk. • Season the soup with the salt, pepper, sugar and cardamom and serve at once. Dust a little cinnamon powder onto the soup, if desired.

Pepper and Sweetcorn Soup

1 each green, yellow and red peppers
25g/1oz vegetable cooking fat
750ml/1¹/₄ pints vegetable stock
400g/14oz pork fillet
1 small onion
4 tbsps oil
400g/14oz canned sweetcorn
2 tsps cornflour
2 generous pinches freshly ground white pepper
2 bunches chives
100g/4oz crème fraîche

Preparation time:
40 minutes
Nutritional value:
Analysis per serving, approx.
• 2400kJ/570kcal
• 25g protein
• 40g fat
• 30g carbohydrate

Wash the peppers, dry, remove the white pith, stalk and seeds and cut into 3cm/1-inch squares. • Melt the vegetable cooking fat in a large saucepan and fry the peppers stirring frequently. Add the vegetable stock and simmer gently for 15 minutes. • Rinse the pork, pat dry and cut into cubes. • Peel and chop the onion. • Heat the oil in a frying pan and fry the pork and onion until brown, stirring frequently. Set aside. • Add the sweetcorn to the peppers and vegetable stock and warm through. • Mix the cornflour with a little cold water and the pepper. • Rinse the chives and chop. • Stir the cornflour and crème fraîche into the soup, bring quickly to the boil and then remove from the heat. • Heat the pork through again. • Add the pork and onion to the soup, garnish with chopped chives and serve.

35

Provençal Vegetable Soup with Pistou

Quantities for 6 people:
3 onions
500g/1lb 2oz tomatoes
500g/1lb 2oz French beans
250g/8oz potatoes
125g/5oz fresh haricot beans
5 tbsps olive oil
$1^1/2$l/$2^1/2$ pints chicken stock
Bunch of savory
Bunch of basil
2-3 garlic cloves
1 tbsp tomato purée
1 tbsp freshly grated Parmesan cheese
1 tbsp breadcrumbs
Salt and freshly ground white pepper

Preparation time:
40 minutes
Cooking time:
30 minutes
Nutritional value:
Analysis per serving, approx:
• 730kJ/170kcal
• 6g protein
• 7g fat
• 22g carbohydrate

Peel and chop the onions. • Slit the tomato skins and pour over boiling water. Drain, remove the skins and chop coarsely. • Wash, trim and halve the French beans. • Peel and dice the potatoes. • Wash the haricot beans. • Fry the onions in 2 tbsps of olive oil until light brown. Add the tomatoes and fry for a little longer. Add the chicken stock, haricot beans and savory in a bunch. Cover, and simmer for 10 minutes. • Add the French beans and diced potatoes and cook for a further 20 minutes. • Wash the basil, dry and chop finely. Peel the garlic and crush into a paste with the basil, tomato purée, cheese and breadcrumbs. Slowly add the remaining oil to the pistou, stirring well. • Remove the bunch of savory from the soup and discard. Season with salt and pepper and serve the pistou separately.

37

Chive Soup

750g/1lb 10oz chicken meat
2 small carrots
2 leek
150g/5¹/₂oz celery
Small bunch parsley
1 tsp black peppercorns
1¹/₂ tsps salt
2 bay leaves
250g/8oz potatoes
100g/4oz shallots
5 bunches chives
25g/1oz butter
100g/4oz crème fraîche
Freshly ground white pepper

Preparation time:
30 minutes
Cooking time:
3 hours
Nutritional value:
Analysis per serving, approx:
• 1600kJ/380kcal
• 32g protein
• 16g fat
• 25g carbohydrate

Wash the chicken. • Clean, wash and chop the vegetables. Reserve some of the carrots. • Wash the parsley and celery leaves. • Bring 2l/3¹/₂ pints water to the boil. Add the vegetables, herbs, peppercorns, a teaspoon of salt, the bay leaves and the chicken. Cook uncovered for 2¹/₂ hours over a low heat, skimming off any scum. • Peel, wash and chop the carrots and shallots. • Chop the chives. • Melt the butter and briefly fry the vegetables and remaining chopped carrot. • Add the chicken stock and cook gently for 30 minutes. Purée the soup in a blender and stir in the crème fraîche and pepper. Adjust the seasoning and reheat.

Chervil Soup

1 onion
500g/1lb 2oz floury potatoes
50g/4oz butter
500ml/18fl oz chicken stock
500ml/18fl oz milk
200g/7oz chervil
125ml/4fl oz white wine
¹/₂ tsp each salt and freshly
ground white pepper
Pinch freshly grated nutmeg
1 egg yolk
125ml/4fl oz cream

Preparation time:
1 hour
Nutritional value:
Analysis per serving, approx:
• 2100kJ/500kcal
• 14g protein
• 34g fat
• 30g carbohydrate

Peel the onion and potatoes.
• Chop the onion finely.
Fry it in the butter until
transparent. Add the chicken
stock and milk and bring to
the boil. •Wash the potatoes,
cut into slices and cook in the
stock over a low heat for 30
minutes. • Purée the soup in a
blender and return to the pan.
• Wash and dry the chervil.
Remove the leaves. • Add the
chervil leaves with the wine to
the soup and season with the
salt, pepper and nutmeg. •
Whisk the egg yolk with the
cream. Remove the soup from
the heat and thicken with the
egg and cream mixture. Do
not return to the heat after
thickening.

Cream of Pea and Ham Soup

300g/10oz dried green peas
1 smoked ham on the bone
(about 1.5kg/3¹/₂lbs)
1 tsp salt
1 leek
1 large carrot
1 parsley root
75g/3oz streaky bacon
1 large onion
1 tbsp soya oil
4 tbsps cream
Generous pinch each of dried
marjoram and freshly ground
white pepper
4 tbsps chopped cress

Soaking time:
12 hours
Preparation time:
45 minutes
Cooking time:
1¹/₂ hours
Nutritional value:
Analysis per serving, approx:
• 1100kJ/260kcal per person
• 10g protein
• 17g fat
• 18g carbohydrate

Wash the peas in cold water and discard any that are discoloured. • Bring the peas and their soaking water to the boil. Add the knuckle of ham and sufficient water to cover and bring to the boil. Skim off any foam that forms, add the salt, cover, and cook for 1¹/₂ hours. • Trim the leek and cut the white part into 4cm/1¹/₂-inch lengths. • Peel and chop the carrot and parsley root. • When the peas and ham have cooked for an hour, add the chopped vegetables. • Chop the bacon, peel the onion and cut into thin rings. • Heat the oil in a frying pan and gently fry the bacon. When it is transparent, add the onion rings and fry both until crispy. Set aside. • Take the knuckle bone out of the saucepan and strain the liquid. • Stir the cream into the soup, season with marjoram and pepper and heat through again. • Pour the soup into a serving bowl and sprinkle with fried bacon, onion rings and cress.

Chicken Soup with Herb and Egg Garnish

1 boiling fowl weighing
approximately 1kg/2^1/₄lbs
1 onion
^{1}/₂ bay leaf
1 clove
1 bundle pot herbs
^{1}/₂ bunch parsley
100g/4oz mushrooms
15g/^{1}/₂oz butter
2 tbsps chopped chives
For the egg garnish:
1 tsp oil
2 eggs
Salt and freshly ground white
pepper

Preparation time:
30 minutes
Cooking time:
1^1/₂ hours
Nutritional value:
Analysis per serving, approx:
• 870kJ/210kcal
• 25g protein
• 11g fat
• 3g carbohydrate

Rinse the fowl inside and out. Peel the onion and stud it with the bay leaf and clove. • Bring the chicken to the boil covered with water together with the onion, the prepared pot herbs, 1 tsp salt and 1 sprig parsley. Reduce the heat and simmer for 1^1/₂ hours. • Clean the mushrooms, slice finely and fry in the butter for 3 minutes. • For the egg garnish, brush the insides of two cups with oil. Chop the remaining parsley finely and mix with the eggs, salt and pepper. Divide between the cups. Seal these with aluminium foil and allow the mixture to cook in hot water for 20 minutes. • Remove the meat from the chicken. Cut half of it into fine strips for the soup. The remainder can be used another time. • Strain the soup and warm the mushrooms in it. • Warm the plates for the soup. Turn out the cooked egg garnish. Cut it into diamond shapes and divide them between the plates. Pour over the hot soup and garnish with chives.

Beef Consommé with Wholemeal Dumplings

500g/1lb 2oz beef bones
1 bunch potherbs (carrot,
onion, parsnip, leek)
5 black peppercorns
1 whole allspice
1 bay leaf
½ tsp sea salt
1 tbsp chopped parsley
For the dumplings:
100g/4oz finely milled
wholemeal flour
1 pinch sea salt
1 pinch freshly ground black
pepper
2 tbsps olive oil
1 tbsp each soy sauce and
tomato purée
2 eggs
1 tbsp chopped parsley
1 tbsp chopped chives

Nutritional value:
Analysis per serving, approx:
• 1200kJ/290kcal
• 21g protein
• 15g fat
• 19g carbohydrate

Wash the bones. • Clean and rinse the pot herbs. Bring to the boil 1¼/2½ pints water with the bones, spices, and bay leaf. Simmer gently for 3½ hours. • To make the dumplings, mix the flour with the salt, pepper and oil, stirring to obtain a crumbly consistency. Add the soy sauce, tomato purée, the eggs, one at a time and finally the herbs. Allow to prove for 30 minutes. • Strain the stock and return it to the boil. •Make the dough into about 16 dumplings and simmer in the stock for 20 minutes. • Sprinkle the soup with the parsley.

Preparation time:
30 minutes
Proving time:
30 minutes
Cooking time:
3½ hours

Poultry Consommé with Chicken Breast

2 filleted and skinned breasts of chicken
2 small cloves garlic
2 tbsps dry sherry
1 tbsp soy sauce
250g/8oz fennel
1l/1³/4 pints chicken stock
¹/2 tsp each salt and freshly ground white pepper

Preparation time:
15 minutes
Marinading time:
30 minutes
Cooking time:
45 minutes
Nutritional value:
Analysis per serving, approx:
• 480kJ/110kcal
• 19g protein
• 1g fat
• 5g carbohydrate

Cut the chicken breast into fine strips. • Peel the garlic cloves and crush with a press into a bowl. Add the sherry and the soy sauce and stir well.• Put the chicken into the marinade, cover and leave to stand in the refrigerator for 30 minutes. • Clean the fennel, rinse thoroughly and pat dry. Reserve the green stemmed portion. Cut the fennel in half lengthways and then into fine strips crosswise. • Bring the chicken stock to the boil. • Simmer the fennel, the strips of chicken breast and the marinade in the stock for 10 minutes over a low heat. • Season to taste with salt and pepper. • Chop the reserved green parts of the fennel and scatter over the soup.

Poultry Consommé with Turkey Breast

¹/₂ bunch mint
1 onion
1 tbsp butter
1l/1³/₄ pints poultry stock
100g/4oz green beans
1 tsp freshly ground white pepper
1 pinch cayenne pepper
6 tbsps couscous
200g/7oz smoked turkey breast cut into thin strips

Preparation time:
40 minutes
Nutritional value:
Analysis per serving, approx:
• 540kJ/130kcal
• 13g protein
• 3g fat
• 2g carbohydrate

Wash the mint. Reserve a few leaves and chop the remainder coarsely. Peel the onion and chop finely. • Melt the butter in a heavy saucepan. Fry the mint and onion lightly. Add the poultry stock and simmer over a low heat for 20 minutes. • Clean and rinse the beans. Chop them finely. Strain the soup through a sieve and return to the pot. Season with the salt, white pepper and cayenne. Add the green beans and the couscous. Simmer the stock for a further 10 minutes, stirring constantly. • Cut the turkey breast into very thin strips. Simmer these in the soup until they are warm •Serve the consommé in soup plates or bowls, garnished with the reserved mint leaves.

Chicken and Banana Soup

1 small chicken (about 1kg/2¼lbs)
1½ tsps salt
8 whole allspice
4 cloves
1 bunch of pot herbs (onion, leek, parsnip, carrot)
100g/4oz long-grain rice
1 firm and 2 soft bananas
1 tbsp curry powder
2 pinches ground ginger
3 tbsps butter
4 tbsps flour
2 tbsps flaked almonds
4 tbsps whipping cream

Preparation time:
30 minutes
Cooking time:
1½ hours
Nutritional value:
Analysis per serving, approx:
- 2500kJ/600kcal
- 30g protein
- 30g fat
- 55g carbohydrate

Wash the chicken and simmer for 30 minutes in 1½l/2½ pints water, containing a teaspoon of salt, the allspice and cloves. Skim off any froth. • Rinse and chop the pot herbs coarsely and add to the stock. • Leave the soup to simmer for a further 45 minutes. • Bring 1l/1¾ pints water to the boil with the rest of the salt. Wash the rice and add to the boiling water. Cook for 20 minutes and allow to drain. • Leave the chicken to cool and then remove the skin and bones. Chop the chicken flesh into small pieces. • Strain the stock. • Mash the soft bananas and stir in the curry powder and ground ginger. • Melt the butter, add the sifted flour and fry until golden brown. Mix with the banana purée and stir into the strained stock. • Reheat the soup and warm through the chicken and rice. • Toast the flaked almonds in a dry frying pan until golden. Whip the cream until stiff. • Serve garnished with firm, banana slices, top with whipped cream and sprinkle with toasted almonds.

46

Hungarian Goulash Soup

500g/1lb 2oz shoulder of beef
250g/8oz onions
1 bundle of pot herbs (carrot,
turnip, onion, celery)
500g/1lb 2oz tomatoes
2 green peppers
2 tbsps pork dripping
1 tsp each salt and paprika
Pinch each freshly ground
caraway seeds and dried thyme
5 tbsps dry white wine

Preparation time:
40 minutes
Cooking time:
1¹/₂ hours
Nutritional value:
Analysis per serving, approx:
• 1300kJ/310kcal
• 28g protein
• 13g fat
• 11g carbohydrate

Rinse the meat, pat dry and remove any fatty tissue or tendons. Cut into cubes. • Peel the onions and cut into rings. Halve each ring. • Rinse and trim the pot herbs and then chop coarsely. • Peel the tomatoes and quarter them. • Wash and dry the peppers. Remove the stalks, white pith and seeds and cut into strips. • Melt the dripping, fry the onions until golden brown and then add the beef. Fry it gently in its own juice for 10 minutes, stirring frequently. • Add the salt, paprika, caraway seeds and thyme and fry for a little longer. Add the pot herbs, tomatoes, peppers and 750ml/1¹/₄ pints of water. Cover and simmer for 1 hour. • Season the soup again with the herbs and wine and serve.

Oxtail Soup with Vegetables

1kg/2¹/₄lbs oxtail in pieces
2 tbsps pork dripping
2 tbsps flour
1¹/₂l/2¹/₂ pints beef stock
1 bay leaf
2 cloves
10 black peppercorns
500g/1lb 2oz each celery
heart, carrots and potatoes
250g/8oz each onions and
leeks
4 tbsps red wine
Pinch of sugar
Salt (optional)

Preparation time:
30 minutes
Cooking time:
2 hours
Nutritional value:
Analysis per serving, approx:
• 1600kJ/380kcal
• 24g protein
• 15g fat
• 40g carbohydrate

Rinse the oxtail and drain on kitchen paper. • Fry in hot pork dripping. Sift the flour into the pan and brown the meat, stirring well. Add the stock, herbs and spices and simmer for 1¹/₂ hours. • Peel and dice the celery, carrots and potatoes. • Peel the onions and cut into strips. Trim the leeks and cut into rings. • Strain the stock and cook the prepared vegetables in the liquid for 25 minutes. • Remove the flesh from the oxtail bones, return to the stock together with the red wine, sugar and a little salt, if desired.

Fish Consommé with Mussels

750g/1lb 6oz fish trimmings
2 cloves garlic
3 onions
1 bay leaf
1 tsp juniper berries
1 tsp black peppercorns
1 tsp salt
500g/1lb 2oz mussels
15g/¹/₂oz butter
125ml/4fl oz white wine
500g/1lb 2oz tomatoes
¹/₂ bunch dill, chopped

Preparation time:
30 minutes
Cooking time:
1 hour
Nutritional value:
Analysis per serving, approx:
• 970kJ/230kcal
• 32g protein
• 7g fat
• 5g carbohydrate

Rinse the fish trimmings. •
Peel the onions and garlic
cloves. Simmer 2 onions, 1
clove garlic, the fish trimmings,
bay leaf, juniper berries and
black peppercorns gently in
1l/2¹/₂ pints salted water for 1
hour. • Scrub the mussels and
remove the beards. • Chop the
remaining onion and garlic.
Fry in the butter until
transparent. Add the mussels
and the wine, cover and cook
the mussels for 15 minutes. •
Skin the tomatoes and cut into
cubes. • Strain the fish stock
and the liquid in which the
mussels have been cooked.
Pour both into one bowl and
allow the tomatoes to
marinade in this for 5 minutes.
• Add the mussels to the soup.
Garnish the soup with
chopped dill.

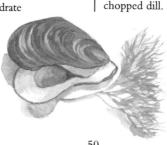

50

Fish Consommé with Garlic Croûtons

500g/1lb 2oz fish trimmings
(head, fins, bones)
1 bunch parsley
2 onions
4 chillies
4 black peppercorns
1 bay leaf
1 tsp salt
250g/8oz fish fillets
1-2 tbsps lemon juice
200g/7oz carrots
1 yellow and 1 red pepper
2 tbsps olive oil
150g/5¹/₂oz shelled peas
1 clove garlic
1 day old bread roll
1 pinch ground white pepper
1 tbsp chopped parsley

Preparation time:
30 minutes
Cooking time:
1¹/₂ hours
Nutritional value:
Analysis per serving, approx:
• 1300kJ/310kcal
• 34g protein
• 9g fat
• 26g carbohydrate

Rinse the fish trimmings. •
Rinse and dry the parsley
and peel the onions. Cut one
onion into quarters and allow
to simmer in 1¹/₂l/2¹/₂ pints
water along with the parsley,
seasonings, the bay leaf, a little
salt and the fish trimmings for
30 minutes. • Sprinkle the
filleted fish with lemon juice. •
Cut the carrots into slices. Cut
the sweet peppers into cubes.
Chop the second onion and fry
it in 1 tablespoon of the oil
until it is transparent. Add the
carrots and 5 tablespoons of
fish stock. Simmer for 5
minutes. Add the cubed
pepper and the peas. Place the
fish fillets over this mixture
and cook for a further 5
minutes. • Peel the garlic
clove, crush, and combine
with the remaining salt. • Cut
the roll into cubes and fry in
the oil with the garlic until
golden brown. Strain the stock
and season with lemon juice
and pepper. Cut up the fish
fillets and add to the soup
together with the vegetables.
Scatter the croûtons and
chopped parsley over the soup.

Crayfish Consommé

250g/8oz live crayfish
2 onions
2 small carrots
2 celery stalks
1 clove garlic
2 tomatoes
50g/2oz butter
$^1/_2$ tsp salt
$^1/_2$ tsp freshly grated white
pepper
1 bay leaf
$2^1/_2$ tbsps cognac
$2^1/_2$ tbsps dry vermouth
$2^1/_2$ tbsps sherry
250ml/8fl oz white wine
750ml/1$^1/_4$ pints chicken stock
150g/5$^1/_2$oz plaice fillet
10 ice cubes
2 sprigs parsley
2 egg whites
$^1/_2$ bunch fresh tarragon
200ml/6fl oz cream
1 egg yolk
1 pinch cayenne pepper
50g/2oz chives

Preparation time:
1 hour
Cooking time:
1$^1/_4$ hours
Nutritional value:
Analysis per serving, approx:
• 2400kJ/570kcal
• 30g protein
• 35g fat
• 16g carbohydrate

Put the crayfish into plenty of boiling water and cook for 2 minutes. Remove from the water and allow to cool. • Peel the onions. Peel the carrots, clean the celery and wash and chop both finely. Peel and crush the garlic. Blanch the tomatoes, skin them and cut into cubes, removing the midribs. • Break off the tails of the crayfish and remove the meat. Remove the coral and reserve with the meat. Remove and discard the hazelnut-sized 'plasticy' gut. •

Place all the shells, the body, tails, legs and pincers in two pieces of foil and crush with a rolling pin. Heat the butter in a saucepan until foaming. Fry the shells, half the vegetables, the garlic, tomatoes, salt, pepper and bay leaf in this, stirring constantly, until they are all lightly browned. • Add the cognac, the vermouth and sherry. Allow to cook briefly. Add the wine and cook for a moment, too. • Add the chicken stock. Simmer for 35 minutes. Switch off the heat and leave to stand for another 30 minutes. •Leave the consommé to cool. Strain it and remove the fat. • Chop the plaice fillets and stir into the pot with the remaining cubed vegetables, the ice cubes, the sprigs of parsley and the egg whites. • Pour on the cooled crayfish consommé and raise the heat while stirring constantly. Simmer gently over a low heat for a further 20 minutes. • Pour boiling water over a muslin cloth. Shake dry and lay on this the tarragon (retaining 2 sprigs of tarragon as a garnish). • Strain the consommé through the muslin. If necessary, season with a little salt and pepper. • Preheat the oven to 250°C/450°F/gas mark 7. • Whip the cream until semi-stiff and fold in the coral, the egg yolk and cayenne pepper. •Divide the crayfish tails between 4 ovenproof cups and fill these with the consommé. Cover each portion with the semi-stiff cream. • Bake in the oven on the top shelf or under an electric grill until the cream is lightly browned. • Garnish the consommé with tarragon and chives.

Our tip: This consommé can also be made with scampi.

Bouillon Mignon

1 plaice
200ml/6fl oz cream
1 bunch dill
2 onions
1 carrot
2 celery stalks
50g/2oz butter
250ml/8fl oz white wine
Freshly ground white pepper
and salt
800ml/1¼ pints beef stock
3 egg whites
1 slice truffle
150g/5½oz prawns

Preparation time:
50 minutes
Cooking time:
1 hour
Nutritional value:
Analysis per serving, approx:
• 1900kJ/450kcal
• 31g protein
• 28g fat
• 12g carbohydrate

Fillet the plaice. Break up its bones • Put the cream and filleted fish in the refrigerator. • Chop the stalks and leaves of the dill finely and set aside. • Chop the vegetables finely. • Melt the butter in a saucepan until foaming. Fry the bones, skin and head of the plaice briefly. Add half of the vegetables and fry for a further 3 minutes. Add the white wine, pepper, a little salt and cook until reduced a little. • Pour on the stock and simmer for 25 minutes. Turn off the heat and leave to stand on the hob for 15 minutes. Then allow to cool. • Cut up the plaice fillets finely. Season them lightly, purée them and stir in one egg white. • Gradually stir in the chilled cream and the dill. Form dumplings from this mixture using 2 teaspoons and simmer over a low heat in salted water for 5 minutes. • Mix well the remaining egg whites and vegetables in a saucepan. Add the stock. Bring to the boil, stirring constantly, and simmer gently over a low heat for 25 minutes. • Cut the truffle into 4 squares. • Strain the stock through a boiled muslin cloth. • Heat the soup bowls. Divide the prawns between them and pour on the stock. Add the dumplings and garnish with the truffle slices.

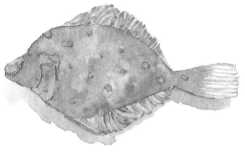

Soupe de Poissons

For the soup:
1kg/2¼ lbs dressed (gutted
and scaled) mixture of fresh
white fish such as cod, hake,
pollack, whiting, coley
250g/8oz peeled prawns
3 onions
1 leek
1 fennel bulb
4 cloves garlic
3 large beefsteak tomatoes
6 tbsps olive oil
2 sprigs fresh thyme
2 bay leaves
2 sachets saffron
1 tsp each salt and freshly
ground white pepper
For the rouille sauce:
1 small dried chilli
3 garlic cloves
2 egg yolks
1 pinch salt
100ml/3fl oz olive oil

To serve:
100g/4oz French bread
50g/2oz freshly grated Gouda
cheese

Preparation time:
50 minutes
Cooking time:
30 minutes
Nutritional value:
Analysis per serving, approx:
• 2100kJ/500kcal
• 44g protein
• 27g fat
• 19g carbohydrate

Chop the fish coarsely.
Wash and drain the
prawns. • Peel and chop the
onions. • Clean and wash the
leek and fennel. Cut into
strips. • Cut the garlic cloves in
half lengthways without
peeling. • Chop the tomatoes

coarsely, removing their midribs. • Heat the oil in a large saucepan and fry the onions until straw coloured. • Fry the fish and prawns for 1 minute. • Add the leek, fennel, garlic, thyme, bay leaf, saffron, salt and pepper and continue cooking for 5 minutes, stirring constantly. Add 2l/3¹/₂ pints boiling water and the tomatoes to the fish, cover and cook over a high heat for 20 minutes. • Strain the soup through a coarse sieve. The vegetables and fish should be rubbed through the sieve as they bind the soup and give it flavour. • Adjust seasoning and keep the soup warm. • To make the rouille, chop the chilli and garlic clove finely. • Whisk the egg yolks and salt in a blender for one minute. Add the chilli and garlic. Add the

oil drop by drop until a creamy mayonnaise is obtained. • Cut the bread into very thin (3mm/¹/₈-inch) slices and toast or bake. • Serve the cheese, soup, toast and sauce separately only bringing them together in the soup plates.

Our tip: The fish soup would be closest to the original if made with small fish from the Mediterranean. Because these are rarely found in the shops and are expensive we have suggested alternatives that are easily obtainable.

57

Green Fish Soup
with Cream

1.2kg/3lbs mixed saltwater
white fish such as pollack, cod
and shellfish
1 carrot
100g/4oz celery
1 onion
1 leek
1 bay leaf
1 tsp white peppercorns
500ml/18fl oz dry white wine
3 egg yolks
250ml/8fl oz cream
Salt and freshly ground white
pepper
1 pinch freshly grated nutmeg
1 tsp lemon juice
$^{1}/_{2}$ tsp Worcestershire sauce
1 bunch each parsley and dill

Preparation time:

1 hour
Nutritional value:
Analysis per serving, approx:
• 3100kJ/740kcal
• 43g protein
• 47g fat
• 14g carbohydrate

Wash the fish. Fillet them and keep the trimmings.
• Peel the carrot, celery and onion and chop coarsely.
Clean and wash the leek and cut into rings. • Add the vegetables, fish trimmings, bay leaf, peppercorns and wine to $^{3}/_{4}$l/1$^{1}/_{4}$ pints water and cook, uncovered, over a high heat for 20 minutes or until reduced by a quarter. • Strain the stock and return to the pan. • Whisk the egg yolks with the cream and stir into the soup. Heat the soup until barely simmering. Do not boil.
• Cut the fish fillets into approximately 4cm/1$^{1}/_{2}$-inch pieces and simmer in the soup for 6 minutes over a very low heat. • Season the soup with the salt, pepper, nutmeg, lemon juice and Worcestershire sauce. • Wash the herbs, dry, chop finely and stir them into the soup.

Cream of Trout Soup with Watercress

600g/1lb 6oz smoked trout
2 shallots
1 small bunch watercress
250ml/8fl oz cream
Salt and freshly ground white pepper
Juice of half a lemon
2 egg yolks

Preparation time:
1¹⁄₂ hours
Nutritional value:
Analysis per serving, approx:
• 2200kJ/520kcal
• 39g protein
• 40g fat
• 3g carbohydrate

S kin the trout. Fillet the fish and set aside. • Peel the shallots and cut into quarters. • Wash and dry the cress. Remove the leaves and reserve a few. Cook the remaining cress with the shallots and the fish trimmings in 1¹⁄₄l/2¹⁄₄ pints water for 40 minutes in an open pan over a low heat.

•Strain the stock. • Cut off some pieces from the trout fillets and reserve as a garnish. Purée the remaining fillets in the blender with the cream. Stir into the stock and simmer gently for a further 10 minutes. • Season the soup lightly with salt, pepper and lemon juice. • Whisk the egg yolks. Remove the soup from the heat and thicken with the egg yolks. •Serve the soup in bowls or soup plates, and garnish with the reserved pieces of trout and cress leaves.

59

Spanish Fish Soup

500g/1lb 2oz beefsteak
tomatoes
1 onion
2 tbsps olive oil
3 cloves garlic
2 tbsps brandy
1 sachet saffron
1 tsp salt
$^1/_2$ tsp freshly ground black
pepper
4 tbsps breadcrumbs
3 small courgettes
400g/14oz fish fillets
150g/5$^1/_2$oz peeled prawns
200g/7oz small clams
$^1/_2$ bunch parsley

Preparation time:
1$^1/_2$ hours
Nutritional value:
Analysis per serving, approx:
• 1200kJ/290kcal
• 35g protein
• 8g fat
• 16g carbohydrate

Blanch the tomatoes. Skin and chop them, removing the midribs. • Peel and chop the onion. Fry it in a large saucepan in the oil until transparent. •Peel and crush the garlic before adding to the onions. Pour on the brandy. • Add the chopped tomatoes, saffron, salt, pepper and breadcrumbs. Add 1l/1$^3/_4$ pints water, cover the pan and simmer over a low heat for 1 hour. •Clean and wash the courgettes, removing their stems, and cut into thin slices. • Wash the fish fillet and cut into approximately 4cm/1$^1/_2$-inch pieces. Add to the soup together with the prawns, washed clams and courgette slices. Allow to simmer for 5 minutes over a low heat. • Wash, dry and chop the parsley. • Adjust the seasoning to taste and sprinkle the soup with the parsley.

Thick Fish Soup

1 onion
150g/5¹/₂oz celery
150g/5¹/₂oz carrots
2 thin leek
250g/8oz floury potatoes
1 clove garlic
2 tbsps butter
¹/₂ tsp each salt and freshly
ground white pepper
3 tsps turmeric
Juice of 1 small lemon
4 tbsps crème fraîche
750g/1lb 10oz mixed fish
fillets
1 bunch dill
1 tsp fennel seeds

Preparation time:
1 hour
Nutritional value:
Analysis per serving, approx:
• 1300kJ/310kcal
• 33g protein
• 11g fat
• 20g carbohydrate

Peel and chop the onion.
Peel and wash the celery
and carrots and chop finely. •
Clean and wash the leek and
cut into rings. • Peel and wash
the potatoes and grate finely. •
Peel and chop the garlic. •
Melt the butter in a large
saucepan. Fry the onion and
garlic until transparent. Then
add the vegetables and sweat
for 5 minutes, stirring
constantly. • Add the spices,
lemon juice and 1l/1³/₄ pints
water. Cover the pan and cook
the soup for 30 minutes over a
low heat. • Purée the soup in a
blender. Return to the heat
and adjust seasoning. Stir in
the crème fraîche. Wash the
fish fillets and cut into
approximately 4cm/1¹/₂-inch
pieces. Simmer them in the
soup for 5 minutes. • Wash
and dry the dill, removing the
leaves. Sprinkle these over the
soup with the fennel seeds.

Cioppino

Quantities for 6 servings
1kg/2¼lbs mussels
750ml/1¼ pints red wine
2 large onions
3 garlic cloves
2 green peppers
600g/1lb 6oz beefsteak
tomatoes
250g/8oz mushrooms
Bunch of basil
8 tbsps olive oil
1½ tsps salt
1 tsp freshly ground white
pepper
75g/3oz tomato purée
750g/1lb 10oz monkfish
fillets
500g/1lb 2oz uncooked king
prawns
Bunch of parsley

Preparation time:
1 hour

Nutritional value:
Analysis per serving, approx:
- 2000kJ/480kcal
- 55g protein
- 14g fat
- 10g carbohydrate

Brush the mussels under running cold water and remove any filaments from around the shells. • Bring half the wine to the boil, add the mussels, cover and cook for 5 minutes. Shake the saucepan frequently to ensure the mussels cook evenly. Pour the contents of the pan through a sieve. • Strain the wine stock through a muslin cloth. • Peel and chop the onions and garlic cloves. • Wash and trim the peppers and then chop them coarsely. Peel the tomatoes and remove the midribs and seeds. • Wipe the mushrooms and cut